Paella-Like It!

Great Ways to Make and Serve Paella

BY

MOLLY MILLS

Copyright © 2020 by Molly Mills

License Notes

No part of this book may be copied, replicated, distributed, sold or shared without the express and written consent of the Author.

The ideas expressed in the book are for entertainment purposes. The Reader assumes all risk when following any guidelines and the Author accepts no responsibility if damages occur due to actions taken by the Reader.

Table of Contents

Introduction 6

Paella-Love It! 9

It's Not Just About Paella 11

Different Paella Recipes 13

    Classic Spanish Paella 14

    Traditional Paella Valenciana 17

    Seafood Paella 20

    Vegetable Paella 23

    The Ultimate Mixed Paella 26

    Spicy Pork and Clam Paella 29

    Shrimp and Chorizo Paella 32

    Squid Ink Paella 35

    Classic Chicken Paella 38

    Turkey Paella 40

    Roasted Peppers and Scallop Paella 42

    Cod and Peas Paella 45

Spicy and Lemony Paella 48

Red Paella 51

Runner Beans and Prawns Paella 54

Fish Broth Paella 57

Quick and Easy Paella 59

Baked Paella 61

Paella Fried Rice 64

Pasta Paella 66

Paella Bites 69

Seafood Paella Soup 71

Paella Accompaniments 74

Spanish Cheese Board 75

Spanish Skewers 77

Spicy Fruit Salad 80

Tomato Bread 82

Spanish Sausage Rolls 84

Caesar Salad 87

Basque Burnt Cheesecake 89

Sangria 92

Conclusion 94

About the Author 95

Don't Miss Out! 96

Introduction

Paella is a communal dish. It is certainly meant to be served straight from the pan. And the diners traditionally would not use a plate but take a spoonful from the pan and take it to their mouths. That's how informal and spontaneous a paella meal is served.

But, of course, to complete the delight of everybody, there have to be other dishes circling the beloved paella pan. While you can always do make with paella and a bottle of good quality wine, it is still much better if you serve it together with other dishes that will complement it perfectly. That's the way to provide everybody a balanced and ultimately satisfying meal.

So, in this paella cookbook, we are giving you more than just paella recipes. As a star of the show, however, it will take the center stage, still. But the recipes of other accompaniments will be present as well to give you an idea of how to present and impress with a full-on Spanish dinner! Let's take a sneak peek of the recipe lineup:

Different Paella Recipes:

- Classic Spanish Paella
- Traditional Paella Valenciana
- Seafood Paella
- Vegetable Paella
- The Ultimate Mixed Paella
- Spicy Pork and Clam Paella
- Shrimp and Chorizo Paella
- Squid Ink Paella
- Classic Chicken Paella
- Turkey Paella
- Roasted Peppers and Scallop Paella
- Cod and Peas Paella
- Spicy and Lemony Paella
- Red Paella
- Runner Beans and Prawns Paella
- Fish Broth Paella
- Quick and Easy Paella
- Baked Paella
- Paella Fried Rice
- Pasta Paella

- Paella Bites
- Seafood Paella Soup

Paella Accompaniments:

- Spanish Cheese Board
- Spanish Skewers
- Spicy Fruit Salad
- Tomato Bread
- Spanish Sausage Rolls
- Caesar Salad
- Basque Burnt Cheesecake
- Sangria

It's great to have Paella at the dining table and be able to share it with the rest of the family. But it's an even greater feat if you are able to create a full Spanish banquet – with the help of this recipe book, of course.

Paella-Love It!

Paella is the pride of Spanish cuisine, particularly of Valencian cuisine. As years passed, many different versions came, but it is naturally the same thing – a one-pan meal with rice, veggies, and protein cooked and served in one hell of a pan with a lot of oomph (read: spices and seasoning).

Traditional paella originated from Valencia. It is a dish made with rice, rabbit, seafood, and other ingredients. But the special pan is as important as the ingredients you throw in it. A paella pan is usually round and thick and is characterized by a flat bottom. It is also not too deep. There may be bigger pans but never deeper ones. Why, the Spanish love it that the rice has as much contact with the bottom of the pan as possible.

Most paella recipes are cooked over a fire. During ancient times, slow, burning firewood easy does it. These days, however, with several versions of the dish available, some may be cooked in an open fire while others are cooked in the oven or elsewhere.

The ingredients in a paella dish may differ from region to region and from one cook to another. As we said, all paellas are almost the same thing. The choice of ingredients may vary, however, depending on the region, season and cook. A variety of meats, veggies, and seafood may be added into the dish depending on their availability and basically the preference of the cooks and diners.

If you think that's all there is to understanding this special dish, think again. The manner of eating paella is as remarkable as the manner of cooking itself. Traditionally, it is considered a family dish, eaten right from the pan. Everyone only has their spoon on hand and spoons directly to the delight of their tummies.

Cooking and eating paella is so much fun. Factor in how much history is attached to it, and you will appreciate it even more. To see what we mean, you simply have to be creative and look at paella as a playing ground. Whatever you decide to cook in your paella pan, as long as you follow the spice notes, you can't go wrong with it. In fact, you can do wonders with it and wow your crowd with a comforting, delightful dish that will stick into their memories.

It's Not Just About Paella

It is almost irresistible to serve a full-on Spanish meal when you already have paella at the center of the dining table. The extravagance of the dish is a call for celebration in itself.

That's why it is not so difficult to pick accompaniments to paella, from side dishes to salads to drinks and desserts. There are indeed a lot of good options available, and they are quite easy to prepare as well. It's actually quite impossible to go wrong.

Spanish tapas or light meals that are served as appetizers and snacks are your best options to serve alongside paella. They are as much a part of the Spanish dining culture as our main recipe, and it is but right that we give them a fair share of the spotlight as well. Apart from the sides, there are also choice desserts and drink mixes that will essentially enhance the dining experience for everyone. Here are some delectably bright ideas to get you started:

Keep it simple and light. Paella is almost like a meal-in-one. You hardly need a lot of fillers just some foods that you could pick on while you share great conversations with your family.

Serve a salad with flavors that complements that of a paella. With that, Caesar Salad is best suited with its light and fresh demeanor. It simply perfectly fits because it helps to somehow neutralize the heavy meaty taste of the main dish.

Serve sides in really small pieces so your guests will not feel too stuffed.

Skip creamy dessert choices. As with the first note, you have to keep the rest simple because paella is ultimately a fully loaded dish. A serving of fresh fruits with a light syrup will do. If you want to go impressive, you can well do a flan or a Basque burnt cheesecake.

Paella is great for entertaining, and thinking out the drinks to serve will make it even more so. To give out an exciting fine dining feel, white wine, dry sherry or cocktails like a Sangria can easily turn up the mood into good.

Paella is almost like a one-course meal, but if you want to serve other dishes alongside, it's fine. You just have to be picky with your choices, making sure your guests will be impressed instead of bloated; satisfied instead of merely stuffed. Opt for light options, palate cleansers, and, since it is already a handful to prepare a paella dish, easy to make.

Different Paella Recipes

Classic Spanish Paella

This is the ultimate paella dish! If you want the most authentic flavor combinations, the one well-loved by Spanish families for centuries, you should learn this recipe. This is great for entertaining guests, whether you have just this dish or you serve it with a light salad and some crusty bread. Plus, a bottle of red wine, of course!

Serving Size: 8

Prep Time: 45 mins

Ingredients:

- 3 cups Arborio rice
- 1 tsp saffron threads
- 4 pcs skinless and boneless chicken thighs, halved
- 8 pcs jumbo shrimps, peeled, leaving the tails intact
- 8 pcs mussels, rinsed and cleaned
- 6.5 oz Spanish chorizo sausage, sliced into ½ inch thick pieces
- 4 oz prosciutto, diced into 1-in pieces
- 1 cup frozen green peas
- 1 cup red bell pepper, finely chopped
- 1 cup canned diced tomatoes with juices
- 2 cups onion, finely chopped
- 5 cloves garlic, minced and divided
- 1 pc lemon, sliced into wedges
- 1 cup fresh parsley, chopped
- 2 tbsp olive oil, divided
- 1 cup water
- 3 16-oz cans chicken broth
- ½ cup fresh lemon juice, divided
- 1 tsp sweet paprika

Instructions:

Mix together parsley and half of the minced garlic, olive oil, and fresh lemon juice. Stir and set aside.

Meanwhile, stir together water and broth, plus saffron in a saucepan. Simmer on low heat for 10 minutes approximately.

In a paella pan, heat the remaining olive oil on medium high and sauté chicken for about 2 minutes. Remove to a plate and set aside.

Next, brown sausage and prosciutto in the same pan for about 2 minutes. Place in a separate plate and set aside.

Add shrimps to the same pan and cook for 2 minutes.

Reduce heat to medium-low and sauté onions and bell peppers in the same pan for about 15 minutes, stirring often.

Add the tomatoes with all its juices, plus the remaining garlic and some paprika. Stir and cook for about 5 minutes.

Next, add rice and stir constantly for a minute.

Add the herb blend and the simmered broth, plus precooked chicken and sausage mix.

Stir in peas and cook in a low boil for 10 minutes, stirring often.

Place mussels and shrimps into the pan and cook for 5 minutes.

Drizzle the remaining lemon juice on top, turn off fire, and cover the pan with a towel.

Lastly, let it stand for 10 minutes before serving with lemon wedges on the side.

Traditional Paella Valenciana

The Valencian paella may not be the highly favored one, but it is actually the original one. After all, this favorite Spanish recipe originated from Valencia where the word "paella" is a local term for wok, particularly the wok where the dish is cooked in. It all started when rice fields sprouted around the same time the Arabs introduced a way to incorporate rice into their daily meals. Discover what separates the Valencian paella from all the rest. Check out this recipe.

Serving Size: 4

Prep Time: 50 mins

Ingredients:

- 2 ½ cups Bomba rice
- 1 tsp saffron threads
- 1 lb. rabbit, cut into small pieces
- 1 lb. chicken, cut into small pieces
- 10 pcs snails, preboiled
- 1 cup green beans
- 1 cup lima beans
- 1 pc ripe tomato
- 1 tbsp fresh rosemary sprigs
- ½ cup extra virgin olive oil
- 1.5 l chicken stock
- Salt to taste

Instructions:

First, heat oil in a paella pan on medium fire and brown chicken and rabbit for about 5 minutes, stirring frequently.

Stir in tomatoes and green and lima beans, then, sauté for a few minutes.

Gently pour in chicken stock, plus rosemary sprigs.

Once the mixture starts to boil, add rice and snails, plus saffron. Sprinkle with some salt and stir.

Turn up the heat. Let the mixture boil, then turn heat to medium-low and cook everything in a simmer for 10 minutes approximately or until most of the liquid is absorbed.

Serve and enjoy.

Seafood Paella

Everyone's memory of paella is mostly with seafood because naturally, that's the first thing you will see because they accentuate the top view of the pan. In reality, however, there is as much meat in the dish as there is seafood. It's a different case with this particular recipe, however, because it's really just seafood. No fancy meat for carnivores. But it's the same great-tasting paella. As long as there are rice and saffron, it's good paella, as they say!

Serving Size: 6

Prep Time: 1 hr.

Ingredients:

- 2 cups jasmine rice
- 1 tsp saffron threads
- 21 oz shrimps
- 12 pcs mussels, rinsed and cleaned
- 8 oz squid rings
- ½ cup frozen peas
- ½ cup dry white wine
- 1 pc red bell pepper, diced
- 2 tbsp flat leaf parsley, chopped
- 4 pcs tomatoes, chopped
- 1 pc onion, chopped
- 3 ¾ cups chicken broth
- 6 cloves garlic, finely chopped
- 2 tbsp olive oil
- ½ tsp garlic powder
- ½ tsp onion powder
- 1 tsp sweet paprika
- Salt and pepper to taste

Instructions:

First, heat oil in a paella pan on medium fire and sauté garlic, onion, and bell pepper for about 3 minutes.

Stir in chicken and cooked for about 5 minutes until lightly browned.

Add tomatoes and stir. Sprinkle with some paprika, onion and garlic powders, plus salt and pepper to taste and cook for about 5 minutes.

Next, toss in mussels and squid rings and cook for another 5 minutes.

Add rice, peas, and saffron, plus chicken broth. Stir to combine and boil, then, reduce heat to low and cook until most of the liquid is absorbed.

Stir in shrimps and cook for about 5 minutes more or until the shrimps are bright orange and the rice is cooked through.

Lastly, serve with a garnish of freshly chopped parsley on top.

Vegetable Paella

Those who are certainly following a special diet or are simply not fond of meat should rejoice because there is a paella variant they can turn to. This one's great for vegetarian diners. There's no meat in it, but it's as equally delicious as the rest.

Serving Size: 6

Prep Time: 1 hr. 15 mins

Ingredients:

- 2 cups short-grain brown rice
- ½ tsp saffron threads, crumbled
- 1 14-oz can artichokes, quartered
- 2 pcs red bell peppers, seeded and sliced into strips
- 1 15-oz can chickpeas, rinsed and drained
- ½ cup frozen peas
- 1 pc lemon, sliced into wedges
- 1 15-oz fire-roasted diced tomatoes, drained
- 1 pc yellow onion, finely chopped
- 6 cloves garlic, minced
- 2 tbsp lemon juice
- 3 tbsp extra-virgin olive oil, divided
- 3 cups vegetable broth
- ½ cup Kalamata olives, pitted and halved
- ⅓ cup dry white wine
- ¼ cup fresh parsley, chopped
- 2 tsp smoked paprika
- 1 ½ tsp fine sea salt, divided
- Freshly ground black pepper to taste

Instructions:

Preheat the oven to 350 degrees F. Then, arrange the oven racks, one at the upper thirds and another at the lower thirds.

Meanwhile, heat about 2 tablespoons of oil in a paella pan on medium fire and sauté the onions with a pinch of salt. Then, stir until the onions are translucent, about 5 minutes.

Stir in the garlic and paprika and cook for another 2 minutes.

Add tomatoes and cook for 2 minutes more, stirring often.

Stir in rice, saffron, chickpeas, wine, and broth. Season with about a teaspoon of salt.

Next, turn up the heat to medium high and let the mixture boil.

Cover the pan with a tight-fitting lid and place onto the lower rack of the preheated oven. Bake for about 50 minutes.

Meanwhile, toss the bell peppers, artichokes, olives, a tablespoon of olive oil and some salt in a rimmed baking sheet lined with baking paper. Spread out the veggies evenly and place the baking sheet at the upper rack. Roast for about 40 minutes.

Add parsley and lemon juice into the roasted veggies and toss again to combine. Set aside.

When the paella is done, sprinkle the peas and roasted veggies on top, then, transfer to the stove over medium-low. Cook for 5 minutes more.

Lastly, Allow it to sit for a few minutes and serve with a garnish of freshly chopped parsley on top.

The Ultimate Mixed Paella

What if you all love meat, seafood, and veggies with your paella? Well, this is the answer. It's the ultimate paella dish with all ingredients possible. You can always pick anything in season, anything that's available and throw it into the paella pan. It will still taste as delightful, promise!

Serving Size: 6

Prep Time: 2 hrs. 20 mins

Ingredients:

- 3 cups short grain Spanish rice
- ½ tsp saffron
- 5 lb. chicken, cut up into **Serving** pieces
- 2 pcs lobsters, boiled, split and divided into sections
- 8 pcs king crab claws
- 1 lb. medium shrimp, shelled
- 18 pcs clams
- ¼ lb. chorizo, cut into ¼-inch slices
- ¼ lb. Jamón Serrano ham, diced
- 2 pcs roasted piquillo peppers
- 4 pcs scallions, chopped
- 1 pc onion, peeled
- 1 pc onion, chopped
- 4 cloves garlic, finely chopped
- 6 tbsp parsley, chopped and divided
- 2 pcs bay leaves, crumbled
- 1 pc lemon, sliced into wedges
- ¼ tsp smoked Spanish paprika
- ½ cup olive oil
- 6 cups chicken broth

Instructions:

Preheat the oven to 325 degrees F.

Stir together saffron, paprika, broth, and whole, peeled onion in a stockpot. Boil over medium fire for about 15 minutes.

Meanwhile, sprinkle salt on chicken pieces and massage gently to season.

Heat oil in a paella pan and brown the chicken pieces until nicely golden. Remove to a plate and set aside.

Next, in the same pan, add the sliced chorizo and diced ham and stir for about 10 minutes. Transfer to another plate and set aside.

Sauté the onions, garlic, scallions, and roasted peppers until fragrant.

Stir in shrimps and boiled lobsters for about 3 minutes. Place the shrimps and lobsters into the plate with the browned chicken pieces.

Add rice into the pan and mix to coat with oil.

Stir in most of the parsley, plus bay leaves and add boiled spiced broth. Season with salt and mix to combine.

Next, cook for about 10 minutes or until the rice is cooked through.

Place back all the precooked ingredients into the pan, together with the clams, burying them deep into the rice.

Place the paella pan into the preheated oven and bake for 20 minutes without cover.

Then, cover the top loosely with foil and place in the stove on medium fire for about 10 minutes.

Lastly, serve with a garnish of freshly chopped parsley and lemon wedges.

Spicy Pork and Clam Paella

Here is a nicely seasoned meat and seafood paella that's great for entertaining guests. It's a delicious mix of pork, chorizo and clams, which can easily brighten up the dining table with delight. This is great, whether you simply want to entice your family with a delicious weeknight meal or you need to impress friends and family during a special dinner.

Serving Size: 6

Prep Time: 1 hr.

Ingredients:

- 2 cups paella rice
- ½ tsp saffron
- 1 lb. pork leg, cut into chunks
- ½ lb. clams, cleaned and rinsed
- ½ lb. chorizo sausage, cut into small pieces
- ½ lb. baby spinach
- 1 14-oz can cherry tomatoes
- 1 pc onion, finely chopped
- 2 cloves garlic, sliced
- 1 tbsp smoked paprika
- 4 tbsp olive oil, divided
- 1 l vegetable stock, warmed

Instructions:

First, in a paella pan, heat 2 tablespoons of olive oil on medium-high and brown pork pieces for about 5 minutes. Transfer to a bowl and set aside.

Second, add the remaining oil in the same pan and sauté the onions and garlic, plus chorizo. Cook for 5 minutes, stirring frequently, until fragrant.

Stir in rice, saffron, and paprika for about 2 minutes until rice is well coated in oil.

Pour the cherry tomatoes, including all its juices, then, put back the browned pork pieces.

Add most of the vegetable stock and let it boil for about 5 minutes, then cook in a simmer for about 15 minutes until most of the liquid is absorbed and the rice is cooked.

Then, arrange clams and spinach on top of the pan. Pour the reserved stock. Let cook for another 10 minutes.

Serve and enjoy.

Shrimp and Chorizo Paella

There is nothing like delicious shrimp and chorizo paella. The balance of flavors, from fresh seafood and some cured meat, create an exciting adventure in the palate. This one is like the classic paella with the classic flavors, a sure crowd pleaser that is so easy to Prepare; you can actually whip it up on weeknights and impress everyone alright.

Serving Size: 6

Prep Time: 30 mins

Ingredients:

- 1 ½ cups Arborio rice
- 1 tsp saffron threads
- 1 lb. shrimps
- 8 oz Spanish chorizo, sliced into rounds
- 1 pc onion, diced
- 4 cloves garlic, minced
- 1 tbsp parsley, chopped
- 2 tbsp tomato paste
- 2 tbsp olive oil
- 3 cups chicken stock
- 1 tsp smoked paprika
- ½ tsp red chili flakes
- ½ tsp turmeric
- 1 tsp kosher salt

Instructions:

First, heat oil in a paella pan over medium fire and sauté the onions for about 5 minutes.

Next, stir in garlic. Cook for another minute.

Add tomato paste, stirring occasionally, and cook for 2 minutes more.

Sprinkle saffron, paprika, turmeric, chili flakes, and salt and stir to blend.

Next, add rice and stir until well coated in grease and spices.

Gently pour stock and boil, then, reduce heat to low and cook rice in a simmer for about 10 minutes.

Arrange the chorizo slices on top and cover. Cook for another 5 minutes.

Place the shrimps on top and press gently into the rice. Cook for 5 minutes more until the shrimps are bright orange and much of the liquid is absorbed.

Lastly, serve with a garnish of freshly chopped parsley.

Squid Ink Paella

Paella Negra or a dark version of the dish is another sought after recipe that you must learn and be prepared with for special family dinners. It looks great and tastes wonderful, too. Thanks to the inclusion of squid ink, you can easily prepare a seemingly exotic dish for your family.

Serving Size: 6

Prep Time: 1 hr. 20 mins

Ingredients:

- 12 oz Bomba rice
- Pinch of saffron
- ½ cup squid ink
- ½ lb. squid, cleaned and sliced into rings
- 1 lb. prawns
- 2 pcs plum tomatoes, chopped
- 1 pc white onion, finely chopped
- 8 cloves garlic, finely chopped
- 1 pc lemon, sliced into wedges
- ¼ cup parsley, chopped
- ½ cup Chardonnay
- ¼ cup extra virgin olive oil
- 6 cups fish stock
- 1 tsp sweet paprika
- ½ tsp salt

Instructions:

First, heat oil in a paella pan. Add squid. Sauté for 30 seconds, then, remove to a plate and set aside.

In the same pan, sauté the onions and cook for 5 minutes, until fragrant.

Next, add garlic and tomatoes and cook for another 5 minutes.

Sprinkle saffron and paprika, reduce heat to low, and simmer for about 10 minutes.

Stir in rice until well coated with tomato mixture.

Add wine and simmer for about 5 minutes.

Pour in stock and squid ink, season with salt, and stir.

Next, turn up the heat to medium until the rice is boiling, then, turn back to low and cook in a gentle simmer for about 0 minutes or until much of the liquid is absorbed. Stir occasionally to ensure the bottom is not burnt.

Arrange the prawns neatly on top of the rice and cook for another 5 minutes.

Place back the cooked squid, then, turn off the heat.

Let the dish rest for 10 minutes. Then, garnish with freshly chopped parsley and lemon wedges.

Serve and enjoy.

Classic Chicken Paella

If you truly want to go back to basics, then chicken paella is your best bet. This is a no frills recipe because the ingredients are accessible and affordable. Most of them are readily found in the pantry. And best of all, you may substitute the ingredients depending on what's within reach or what produce is in season.

Serving Size: 6

Prep Time: 1 hr. 10 mins

Ingredients:

- 1 ¼ lb. Paella rice
- 30 pcs saffron threads, soaked in hot water
- 2 2/3 lb. chicken, sliced into chunks
- 1 lb. green beans, nicely cut into 2-inch pieces
- 11 oz butterbeans
- 3 pcs tomatoes, crushed
- 2 pcs rosemary sprigs
- ½ cup extra virgin olive oil
- 11 cups water
- Salt to taste

Instructions:

Heat oil in a paella pan over medium fire.

Brown chicken chunks in hot oil for about 20 minutes, stirring occasionally.

Add green beans and butterbeans.

Stir in tomatoes and let cook for a few more minutes.

Add rice, saffron, and the rest of the ingredients. Stir to blend.

Let it boil on high heat, then, turn to low and simmer until much of the liquid is absorbed.

Set aside for a few minutes before **Serving** with more rosemary sprigs sprinkled on top.

Serve and enjoy.

Turkey Paella

You want a quick and easy paella? We hear ya! This turkey paella is perfect for weeknight dinners when you still want to make sure your family is served with a hearty meal no matter how busy the day has been. This one gets done in 20 minutes, with very simple ingredients, and it tastes w-o-w all the same.

Serving Size: 4

Prep Time: 25 mins

Ingredients:

- 1 20-oz jar paella paste
- 2 ½ cups paella rice
- ½ lb. roast turkey slices, torn into pieces
- 12 oz stir-fry vegetable mix
- 2 tbsp extra virgin olive oil, divided
- 8 cups hot water
- Salt and pepper to taste

Instructions:

Heat 1 tablespoon of oil in a paella pan on medium fire and sauté the jarred paella paste for about 2 minutes.

Add rice and stir to coat. Then, pour in water. Let it boil and turn heat to low to cook in a simmer for 15 minutes.

Next, in another pan, heat the remaining oil on medium-high and fry the veggies for about 2 minutes. Season with some salt and pepper, then, turn off the fire.

Scatter the veggie mix and torn roast turkey onto the paella pan, spreading evenly.

Lastly, serve and enjoy.

Roasted Peppers and Scallop Paella

You want something that is sweet and savory at the same time? Here's a good recipe for you to tinker with. It's loaded with roasted bell peppers, artichoke, and scallops. Plus, there's a slight kick of spice with some green chilies thrown into the equation. This is an impressive dinner treat, whichever way you look at it.

Serving Size: 6

Prep Time: 1 hr.

Ingredients:

- 1 ½ cups rice
- ¼ tsp saffron
- 1 pc roasted red bell pepper, cut into strips
- 1 lb. scallops
- 1 6-oz can mild green chilies
- 1 14-oz can artichoke hearts, drained
- 1 pc lemon, sliced into wedges
- 1 pc onion, chopped
- 2 cloves garlic, minced
- 2 tbsp fresh lemon juice
- 3 ¼ cups fish broth
- ¼ cup olive oil, divided
- Salt and ground black pepper to taste

Instructions:

First, heat half of the oil in a paella pan on medium-high fire.

Add scallops and sauté for about 3 minutes, stirring constantly.

Transfer the scallops to a bowl and discard the pan juices.

Put back the pan into the stove and heat the remaining oil over medium fire.

Sauté onion and garlic until fragrant, about 5 minutes.

Stir in rice and sauté for another 5 minutes.

Next, pour in broth, then, sprinkle saffron, salt, and freshly ground black pepper.

Stir and simmer for about 10 minutes approximately or until much of the liquid is absorbed and the rice is cooked.

Stir in most of the roasted bell peppers and chilies (reserving some for garnish), then, cook for another 10 minutes on medium-low.

Put back the scallops into the pan, plus artichoke hearts, and stir. Cook for 5 minutes more.

Garnish top with the remaining bell peppers and chilies.

Serve and enjoy.

Cod and Peas Paella

Here is an easy-peasy paella recipe that will allow you to give your family a great load of nutrients they will need for an instant energy boost. And yes, it is oh-so tasty, you will never get a no for it. There are cod, peas and peppers. It tastes familiar, much like most home-cooked meals.

Serving Size: 2

Prep Time: 55 mins

Ingredients:

- 1 ½ cups brown basmati rice
- 1 tsp saffron threads
- 1 lb. skinless cod, sliced into chunks
- 1 ¼ cups frozen peas
- 1 pc roasted red bell pepper, seeded and chopped
- 1 pc courgetti, diced
- 1 pc onion, finely chopped
- 2 cloves garlic, chopped
- ½ pc lemon, sliced into wedges
- ⅓ cup parsley, chopped
- 1 tbsp grapeseed oil
- 2 ½ cups vegetable stock
- 1 tsp turmeric
- 1 tsp smoked paprika

Instructions:

Heat oil in a paella pan on medium-high and sauté the onions and garlic for a few minutes until softened.

Stir in rice, saffron, turmeric, paprika, salt, and pepper. Stir until rice is well coated in grease.

Gently pour in stock and stir to blend.

Boil and cover. Then, reduce the heat to low. Cook in a simmer for about 20 minutes.

Add courgetti and let cook for another 10 minutes until much of the liquid is absorbed.

Turn up heat to medium. Stir in cods and peas to incorporate.

Leave for a few minutes to rest. Then, serve with a garnish of freshly chopped parsley and lemon wedges.

Spicy and Lemony Paella

Got a party for yuppies? If it's a no-kid event, you can well **Prep**are this tasty spicy paella recipe. The slight hint of kick can be reduced or increased, depending on how brave you and your guests are with the heat. And, indeed, that's not the only great thing about this dish. You can also play around with the other ingredients, depending on what's available and what you like, actually.

Serving Size: 8

Prep Time: 1 hr. 10 mins

Ingredients:

- 2 cups Arborio rice
- 24 pcs large shrimps, peeled and deveined, the tails intact
- 7 oz Andouille sausages, sliced into ½-inch pieces
- 1 cup corn kernels
- 2 cups zucchini, sliced
- 2 ½ cups red bell pepper, finely chopped
- 1 cup diced tomatoes, undrained
- 2 cups onion, finely chopped
- 5 cloves garlic, minced and divided
- ½ cup fresh cilantro, chopped
- 1 pc lime, sliced into wedges
- 2 16-oz cans chicken broth
- ¼ cup fresh lime juice
- 2 tbsp olive oil, divided
- 1 tsp hot paprika
- ¼ tsp salt

For the Broth:

- 1 pc dried New Mexican chili, seeded
- 1 tsp ground cumin
- ½ tsp ground cinnamon
- 2 cloves garlic, peeled

Instructions:

First, make the broth. Put the entire ingredients in a food processor, except for the broth. Pulse until smooth.

Transfer spice blend to a stockpot together with chicken broth and simmer on medium fire to keep warm.

Meanwhile, stir together freshly chopped cilantro and half of the minced garlic with lime juice and 1 tablespoon of olive oil. Set aside.

Next, heat the remaining tablespoon of oil in a paella pan and brown the sausages for about 3 minutes. Transfer to a bowl and set aside.

Add the shrimps into the same pan and stir until they turn bright orange. Place in another bowl and set aside.

Sauté the red bell peppers and onions in the same pan for about 5 minutes or until softened.

Stir in zucchini and cook for another 5 minutes.

Pour in diced tomatoes together with all the juices, then, sprinkle the remaining garlic, paprika, and salt.

Next, add rice to the pan, stirring to coat with the grease.

Stir in warmed broth, the herb blend, corn, and sausages. Cook covered for 10 minutes approximately, stirring occasionally.

Arrange the browned shrimps on top and let cook in low fire for another 10 minutes.

Set aside to rest a little before serving with lime wedges.

Red Paella

So, here is another paella recipe that looks interesting. It's bright red and quite flavorful, with roasted peppers and all. It's also very aromatic, with the delicious spice blend highlighted with garlic and paprika. Let's start making the recipe. You will soon find out what to cook it for.

Serving Size: 6

Prep Time: 1 hr.

Ingredients:

- 3 cups rice
- ¼ tsp saffron
- 12 oz shrimps, peeled and deveined, tails intact
- 8 oz clams, scrubbed and rinsed
- 1 cup roasted sweet red bell pepper, sliced
- 1 pc lemon, sliced into wedges
- 1 pc onion, chopped
- 3 cloves garlic, minced
- ¾ cup olive oil
- 3 ¼ cups fish broth
- 6 ¼ cups chicken broth
- ½ tsp Spanish paprika
- Salt and pepper to taste

Instructions:

First, heat oil in a paella pan on medium high and sauté the onions and bell peppers until softened, stirring occasionally.

Add garlic. Then, cook for 5 minutes more.

Next, stir in rice until well coated in oil.

Add the shrimps, clams, saffron, paprika, salt, and pepper.

Gently pour broth and let it boil, then turn heat to medium and cook for 5 minutes with cover, until much of the liquid is absorbed.

Let it rest for about 5 minutes before serving.

Runner Beans and Prawns Paella

One of the most amazing things about paella is it is quite spontaneous. You can do make with only a few ingredients, but you can also impress with a lot. You can also make choices on what to put into your dish, depending on what's in season or readily accessible to you. As long as you actually have rice and saffron, it will taste like paella alright. For this particular recipe, we are making a perfect pair with runner beans and prawns and chicken meat, if you can't do make without meat.

Serving Size: 4

Prep Time: 40 mins

Ingredients:

- 2 ½ cups paella rice
- 1 tsp saffron
- 3 cups runner beans, trimmed and sliced
- 1 lb. large king prawns
- 8 pcs skinless chicken thighs, sliced into chunks
- 1 pc red bell pepper, nicely seeded and chopped
- 2 pcs onions, chopped
- 4 cloves garlic, sliced
- 1 tbsp sweet paprika
- 2 tbsp olive oil
- 1 cup dry white wine
- 8 cups chicken stock, warmed

Instructions:

Heat oil in a paella pan over medium high and sauté the onions and garlic until fragrant.

Add chicken chunks and cook for another 5 minutes.

Stir in rice, saffron, and paprika until well coated.

Pour in wine and let it sizzle.

Add stock and let it simmer for about 15 minutes until the rice is almost cooked.

Stir in beans and bell peppers and cook for another 5 minutes.

Arrange prawns on top, cover and cook for 5 minutes more. Season with salt and pepper.

Serve and enjoy.

Fish Broth Paella

If you want a money-saving paella, this is a great choice. You can simply cook rice in fish broth and add a few other ingredients, and you are good to go. Of course, you can always add more. But cooking this dish according to the recipe won't hurt. It tastes great all the same. The richness of the broth is good enough.

Serving Size: 10

Prep Time: 53 mins

Ingredients:

- 4 cups Bomba rice
- 1 tsp saffron
- 2.5 l fish broth
- 2 ½ lb. Mediterranean rock fish, sliced into chunks
- 2 lb. potatoes, nicely peeled and diced
- 1 tbsp sweet pepper, diced
- 2 pcs tomatoes, grated
- 4 cups onion, finely chopped
- 3 tbsp olive oil
- Salt and pepper to taste

Instructions:

Heat oil in a paella pan on medium-high and sauté the potatoes, onions, and garlic for about 5 minutes.

Add tomatoes, sweet peppers, and fish broth. Season with saffron, salt and pepper.

Pour in broth and add rice. Let it boil and cover to cook the rice, until much of the liquid is absorbed.

Add fish chunks and cook for another 10 minutes in low heat.

Quick and Easy Paella

If you think paella is always a pain in the back to **Prep**are, think again. There are also recipes that will not require you to tire too much so you can easily enjoy the dish. Here is a 15-minute paella dish so you can better grasp what we mean. Let's do this!

Serving Size: 6

Prep Time: 15 mins

Ingredients:

- 3 cups basmati rice, pre-cooked
- Pinch of saffron
- 3 pcs roasted chicken breasts, skinned and shredded using two forks
- 1 lb. frozen seafood cocktail mix, thawed and rinsed
- 2 cups frozen peas
- 3 pcs roasted red bell peppers in oil, diced
- 1 cup black olives, pitted and halved
- ½ cup fresh parsley, chopped
- 1 pc lemon, sliced into wedges
- 4 cups water

Instructions:

Place water and saffron in a stockpot and boil over medium fire.

Add peas and let cook for about 3 minutes.

Stir in rice, chicken, seafood mix, roasted peppers, and olives until well blended.

Cover. Then, let cook for another minute or more, stirring occasionally.

Toss in half of the parsley, then, transfer to a serving bowl or paella pan, garnish with more parsley plus lemon wedges and serve.

Baked Paella

After the classics come to be the innovative paella recipes, which people came up with to be able to enjoy paella differently. More often, the paella recipes are meant to take away the trouble of preparing the dish that is quite taxing to make. After the quick and easy paella, with most of the ingredients precooked, here is a baked version that will give the dish a twist in texture and prep.

Serving Size: 4

Prep Time: 50 mins

Ingredients:

- 1 lb. Bomba rice
- Pinch of Saffron
- 1 lb. chicken and rabbit joints, sliced into small chunks
- ½ lb. lean pork, sliced into chunks
- 7 oz garbanzo beans, soaked in cold water overnight
- 1 pc red bell pepper, seeded and sliced
- 2 pcs ripe tomatoes, halved crosswise
- 1 pc ripe tomato, grated
- 1 head garlic
- ½ cup olive oil
- 1 qt water
- Pinch of Spanish paprika
- Salt to taste

Instructions:

Preheat the oven to 350 degrees F.

Heat oil in a cast-iron skillet. Then, brown meats until golden.

Add red bell peppers and grated tomatoes. Cook for about 3 minutes, stirring often. Remove to a plate and set aside.

Boil water with saffron and paprika in another pot.

In the same cast iron skillet, arrange rice and the meat and tomato mix, plus garbanzo beans at the bottom.

Gently pour boiling water to cover the entire dish, then, add the whole head of garlic in the middle. Sprinkle some salt.

Tightly Cover with aluminum foil. Then, put in the oven to cook for about 25 minutes.

Remove cover and let cook for another 10 minutes, then, let it rest for 5 minutes.

Serve and enjoy.

Paella Fried Rice

Now, here is another paella version you will surely love. It's fried rice style, which means most of the ingredients are already cooked and will only need to be tossed a few minutes until ready. Believe it or not, it should be ready in 10 minutes! It's a great dish if you suddenly crave Spanish flavors, and you are in a hurry.

Serving Size: 4

Prep Time: 10 mins

Ingredients:

- 4 cups cooked rice
- ½ lb. cooked prawns
- 2 small chorizo sausages, sliced
- 1 cup frozen peas, thawed
- 1 pc lemon, sliced into wedges
- 1 pc onion, sliced
- 1 clove garlic, chopped
- 1 tbsp vegetable oil
- ½ tsp turmeric

Instructions:

Heat oil in a wok and sauté onions, garlic, and chorizo until fragrant.

Sprinkle turmeric, then, add rice, prawns, and thawed peas.

Stir until everything is heated through.

Serve with lemon wedges on the side.

Pasta Paella

Substituting pasta with rice is very common in a lot of recipes. And paella is not exempted. In fact, there is a traditional paella recipe that actually features short pasta, and it is called Fideua. It is packed with all the nice flavors of the usual paella, but instead of rice, it is made with pasta. Believe it or not, it is equally enticing and delightfully good.

Serving Size: 6

Prep Time: 50 mins

Ingredients:

- 12 oz broken spaghetti
- ½ tsp saffron threads
- 1 pc sea bass, deboned and sliced, reserving bones for the stock
- ½ lb. shrimps, shelled but leave the tails on, reserving shells for the stock
- ½ lb. clams, rinsed
- 1 pc carrot, peeled and chopped into pieces
- 1 pc celery stick, chopped
- 1 pc red bell pepper, seeded and diced
- 1 pc onion, sliced and divided
- 3 cloves garlic, minced
- 1 14-oz can crushed tomatoes
- 2 tbsp parsley, chopped
- 1 pc thyme sprig
- ½ tsp fennel seeds
- ½ tsp paprika
- 5 tbsp olive oil
- 4 cups water

Instructions:

Place fish bones, shrimp shells, carrot, celery, parsley, thyme, and half of the onions in a stock pot and heat on medium fire, then, reduce heat to low and cook in a simmer for about 15 minutes.

Meanwhile, heat about 2 tablespoons of oil in a paella pan on medium low and fry the fish and shrimps until almost cooked. Transfer to a plate and set aside.

Add the remaining oil and sauté the remaining onions, plus bell pepper for about 10 minutes.

Stir in garlic, fennel seeds, and paprika.

Add tomatoes, including its juices, and let it cook for 10 minutes, stirring occasionally.

Back to the stockpot, remove the solids and stir in saffron. Let it simmer for 10 minutes more.

Add the pasta to the paella pan and stir to coat with the tomatoes mixture.

Gradually add hot soup stock and then, cook for about 10 minutes.

Stir in clams and cook until they open, then, put back cooked fish and shrimps. Let it cook for about 5 minutes, then, you are ready to serve.

Paella Bites

How about paella in one bite, anyone? This paella version is pretty interesting; It would make an appetizer spread a tad more exciting! That's because guests get to taste paella in full – all its bold flavors and textures – in just one bite. The crispy on the outside leftover paella tidbits would make your Spanish party one to die for.

Serving Size: 4

Prep Time: 40 mins

Ingredients:

- 1 lb. leftover paella
- 4 pcs chorizo, thinly sliced
- 12 pcs green Spanish olives
- 2 pcs eggs, beaten
- ½ cup all-purpose flour
- ¾ cup breadcrumbs
- 1 tsp smoked paprika
- 3 cups vegetable oil

Instructions:

Form paella leftover into 12 balls.

Place flour, eggs, and breadcrumbs together with paprika in separate bowls. Then, dip each paella ball onto flour first, eggs second, and finally coat in spiced breadcrumbs.

Heat oil in a pan or a deep fryer over medium fire until the temperature reaches 350 degrees F.

Fry the coated paella balls until crispy and golden brown.

To serve, skewer each paella ball in a short stick with slices of chorizo and olives on top.

Seafood Paella Soup

One of the many great things about paella is that it can be served in many ways. You can eat it beyond its usual form, as it is with this soup. It's a sticky soup that is known locally as Arroz Caldoso or Seafood Paella Soup. It is bursting with the many bright flavors and colors of paella.

Serving Size: 6

Prep Time: 50 mins

Ingredients:

- 1 lb. short grain Arborio rice
- 12 strands saffron threads
- 10 pcs prawns
- 1 pc crayfish, split in half
- 24 pcs mussels, rinsed
- 6 pcs squid, cleaned and sliced into rings
- ½ lb. cod fish fillet, cubed
- 12 oz sweet pork sausages
- 8 pcs asparagus stalks, sliced into 1-inch pieces
- 2 pcs ripe tomatoes, seeded and finely chopped
- 1 pc lemon, sliced into wedges
- 3 tbsp flat leaf parsley, minced
- 1 pc onion, chopped
- 3 cloves garlic, minced
- 1 pc bay leaf
- 1 cup white wine
- 1 cup fish stock
- 3 tbsp extra virgin olive oil, divided
- 1 tsp salt
- 1/3 tsp black pepper

Instructions:

Add all the seafood in a pot together with stock, white wine, bay leaf, and onion.

Heat on medium-high for about 5 minutes, then, drain, reserving the cooking liquid.

Meanwhile, heat oil in a paella pan over medium fire and brown sausages for about 2 minutes.

Stir in garlic, tomatoes, and rice, then, season with salt and pepper until the rice is well coated.

Add the hot reserved liquid into the pan and cook on medium high for 2 minutes.

Add asparagus and half of the parsley into the mix and reduce heat to low. Simmer for about 15 minutes.

Put back the seafood and let it cook thoroughly for about 5-10 minutes, stirring occasionally.

Add a splash more of stock if the rice becomes too sticky.

Serve with the remaining parsley on top plus lemon wedges on the side.

Paella Accompaniments

Spanish Cheese Board

And then, there are the side dishes that make up a paella meal even more special. To start off, we have this Spanish Cheese Board that is practically complete with intricate elements that you need to start off a meal, any meals for that matter. It's a usual favorite, especially during the holidays, but you can serve it all year round and wow the crowd alright.

Serving Size: 8

Prep Time: 45 mins

Ingredients:

- 6 oz Manchego cheese
- 5 oz Drunken Goat cheese
- 5 oz Iberic cheese
- 3 oz Cabranes cheese
- 1 pc baguette, sliced
- 16 thin Serrano ham slices
- 3 pcs cured chorizo links
- 8 pcs dates, pitted
- 4 cups green and black grapes on the vine
- ¼ cup pickled peppers, drained
- ¾ cup mixed olives, pitted
- 1/3 cup whole almonds, Marconi variety preferred
- 2 cups Romeo sauce
- ¼ cup quince paste
- 1 tbsp sweet smoked paprika

Instructions:

Toss almonds and paprika in a bowl.

Next, arrange your cheese board, following your creativity. You may add other elements according to your liking or their availability.

Serve and enjoy.

Spanish Skewers

Another interesting party appetizer is this skewered treat made with peppers, chorizos and potatoes, served with a special garlic dip. It's as delicious and interesting as it looks, with the bright color combination and bold flavors. Another good thing about this appetizer recipe is that it keeps well in the fridge. You can easily make it ahead of time, so you don't end up haggard when it's time to **Prep**are the rest of your party buffet spread.

Serving Size: 6

Prep Time: 50 mins

Ingredients:

- ½ lb. waxy potatoes, peeled and cut into chunks
- 12 oz chorizo, sliced
- 1 pc yellow bell pepper, deseeded and cut into chunks
- 1 pc red bell pepper, deseeded and cut into chunks
- 1 tbsp olive oil
- 2 tsp fresh rosemary sprigs, finely chopped
- Salt and pepper to taste

For the Garlic Dip:

- 1 clove garlic, crushed
- ½ cup flat-leaf parsley, finely chopped
- 2 cups crème fraiche

Instructions:

Preheat the oven to 350 degrees F.

Meanwhile, boil potatoes in a pan with water until fork tender.

Drain potatoes and toss into a baking sheet with rosemary and oil. Season with some salt and pepper.

Spread potatoes evenly and roast for about 5 minutes, then, stir and add the bell peppers and roast for another 5 minutes.

Thread potatoes, bell peppers, and chorizo slices in a bamboo skewer and place in a parchment paper lined baking tray. Then, cover with a sheet of cling wrap and chip for up to 8 hours.

Meanwhile, make the garlic dip by mixing together garlic, parsley and crème fraiche in a bowl until well blended. Set aside.

When you are ready to serve the skewers, roast them in the oven for about 10 minutes until the veggies are nicely charred and the chorizo sliced are cooked through.

Serve with the Prepared garlic dip on the side.

Spicy Fruit Salad

If you want a less-hassle and healthier appetizer, you can turn into this Spicy Fruit Salad recipe. It's an experience of a lifetime with a pinch of spice sending a serious flavor bomb to explode. You can reduce the spice if you are **Serving** it to young guests, but you can go full blast if you are **Prep**aring for an all-adult party.

Serving Size: 6

Prep Time: 10 mins

Ingredients:

- 2 pcs ripe mangos, peeled and cubed
- 4 pcs medium kiwis, peeled and quartered
- 1 cup strawberries, sliced
- 1 cup blueberries
- 2 tbsp lime juice
- 1 tbsp maple syrup
- 1 oz silver tequila
- ¼ tsp chili powder
- Pinch of sea salt

Instructions:

Stir together tequila, maple syrup, and lime juice in a small bowl.

Toss fruits gently with the tequila mixture, sprinkle with chili powder and salt until well coated.

Cover and chill or serve right away.

Tomato Bread

There are definitely a lot of things to love about Spain, and this recipe of Spanish, tomato bread, is one of them. The recipe is pretty simple, and you need very simple pantry ingredients. But the result is ultimately delicious, a perfect side to your paella and practically every artisan Spanish dish there is.

Serving Size: 6

Prep Time: 15 mins

Ingredients:

- 1 pc ciabatta loaf bread, sliced
- 6 pcs ripe tomatoes, grated
- 2 cloves garlic, peeled and halved
- 1 tsp sea salt
- 2 tbsp olive oil

Instructions:

Broil bread slices for about 2 minutes.

Evenly rub the cut side of the garlic cloves onto the toasted bread.

Divide grated tomatoes evenly among the bread slices, then, drizzle with olive oil and sprinkle with salt.

Serve and enjoy.

Spanish Sausage Rolls

Originally a picnic treat, these Spanish sausage rolls are a common sight. They are easy to make and very convenient to indulge in. They make a nice starter for heavy meals, too. But since we are serving them with paella, we are using spicy chorizo instead of ordinary pork sausage. Dare we say, you will love the difference, most definitely.

Serving Size: 6

Prep Time: 50 mins

Ingredients:

- 12 oz puff pastry
- 1 tbsp flour
- 2 pcs potatoes, peeled and diced
- 12 oz spicy chorizo, skins removed
- ¼ cup parsley, roughly chopped
- 2 tbsp nigella seeds
- 1 pc egg, beaten

Instructions:

In a lightly floured surface, roll out the puff pastry into a rectangle, about 32 x 20 centimeters in size.

Cut the puff pastry in half and arrange in a parchment paper lined baking tray. Set aside in the fridge to chill.

Meanwhile, boil potatoes in a lightly salted water over medium fire until tender, about 5 minutes.

Combine potatoes, chorizo, half of the nigella seeds, plus the parsley in a blender or food processor and pulse until incorporated.

Preheat the oven to 350 degrees F.

Take out the puff pastry and shape into a roll with a spoonful of chorizo mix shaped into sausage in the middle.

Brush the edges of the sausage roll to seal. Cut into about 5 centimeters long each and place in baking trays.

Brush top with more egg, then, sprinkle with the remaining nigella seeds.

Bake for about half an hour approximately until golden brown.

Serve and enjoy.

Caesar Salad

When it comes to **Prep**aring an utterly satisfying meal for a crowd, you can never go wrong by doing classics. Just like this Caesar salad recipe. It is an almost fool-proof dish that will surely please the crowd, especially if you serve it with paella and all its hoopla. It makes for an impressive salad bowl that's screaming fresh in decibels.

Serving Size: 4

Prep Time: 30 mins

Ingredients:

- 1 large romaine lettuce, torn into pieces
- 1 cup croutons
- 1/3 cup parmesan cheese, shredded
- ½ cup Caesar salad dressing

Instructions:

Toss the lettuce and croutons with some dressing, top with shredded parmesan cheese and serve.

Basque Burnt Cheesecake

But, of course, who could have skipped a dessert? No matter how full you could get with all the delicious tapas and the paella itself, you will always have some room for a sweet treat. So, this cookbook comes with one of the most delightful desserts. This is the Spanish's answer to New York's. It's meant to get burnt, cracked, and cooked on high temp.

Serving Size: 6

Prep Time: 1 hr. 10 mins

Ingredients:

- 2 lb. cream cheese, at room temperature
- ⅓ cup all-purpose flour
- 1 ½ cups sugar
- 1 tsp kosher salt
- 1 tbsp unsalted butter
- 6 pcs large eggs
- 2 cups heavy cream
- 1 tsp vanilla extract

Instructions:

First, preheat the oven to 400 degrees F. Place the rack in the middle.

Meanwhile, spread butter in a round pan and place a couple of sheets of parchment paper, overlapping about 2 inches on all the sides. Place the pan in a rimmed baking tray. Set aside.

Beat together cream cheese and sugar on medium-low until smooth and the sugar has completely dissolved.

Next, turn up the speed to medium. Add the eggs one by one, beating about 15 seconds after each addition before the next one.

Put the mixer speed back to low and gradually stir in the heavy cream, vanilla, and salt until incorporated, about half a minute.

Sift flour over the mixture and continue to beat on low for about 15 seconds, scraping the sides as you go.

Then, pour batter onto the prepared pan and bake for about an hour until deeply brown but still jiggly.

Let cool before unmolding, remove the parchment paper, and slice into wedges.

Sangria

To cap off a delicious meal nicely, you need a delicious drink. Here is a classic Spanish sangria to brighten up your party and fill your guests' hearts with joy. It's definitely easy to make and easy to please. You will only need a few minutes and a few ingredients to make it.

Serving Size: 12

Prep Time: 10 mins

Ingredients:

- 2 bottles Spanish red wine
- ½ cup brandy
- ½ cup fresh orange juice
- 1 tbsp maple syrup
- 1 pc green apple, diced
- 1 pc orange, diced
- 1 pc lemon, diced
- 1 pc cinnamon stick

Instructions:

Combine the entire ingredients in a punch bowl or a large pitcher and stir until well blended.

Cover. Set aside in the fridge for at least 30 minutes.

Serve over ice.

Conclusion

Spanish dinners are great. They are filling, hearty, and incredibly delicious. One of the frontrunners of the most memorable Spanish dinners is paella. It is almost like the flagship recipe of Spanish cuisine.

Paella is ultimately a dish on its own. It's a full-on meal. It has carbs, protein, and veggies. And there are many delicious paella versions available. You can substitute ingredients according to your liking and whatever may be available. Seafood paella is a favorite, and so are the recipes with meat.

Even if paella is a meal-in-one, you can never go wrong adding a few recipes to it and make the meal even heartier and more satisfying. That's why we added highly preferred accompaniments, from appetizers to sides and salads to dessert and even a delicious beverage to down it all.

We hope you enjoyed browsing through the many different paella recipes sprouted from all over to give the dish a different take each time. So, you will never have to feel you are just having paella because you can pick a new recipe from this cookbook anytime.

Happy cooking!

About the Author

Molly Mills always knew she wanted to feed people delicious food for a living. Being the oldest child with three younger brothers, Molly learned to prepare meals at an early age to help out her busy parents. She just seemed to know what spice went with which meat and how to make sauces that would dress up the blandest of pastas. Her creativity in the kitchen was a blessing to a family where money was tight and making new meals every day was a challenge.

Molly was also a gifted athlete as well as chef and secured a Lacrosse scholarship to Syracuse University. This was a blessing to her family as she was the first to go to college and at little cost to her parents. She took full advantage of her college education and earned a business degree. When she graduated, she joined her culinary skills and business acumen into a successful catering business. She wrote her first e-book after a customer asked if she could pay for several of her recipes. This sparked the entrepreneurial spirit in Mills and she thought if one person wanted them, then why not share the recipes with the world!

Molly lives near her family's home with her husband and three children and still cooks for her family every chance she gets. She plays Lacrosse with a local team made up of her old teammates from college and there are always some tasty nibbles on the ready after each game.

Don't Miss Out!

Scan the QR-Code below and you can sign up to receive emails whenever Molly Mills publishes a new book. There's no charge and no obligation.

Sign Me Up

https://molly.gr8.com

Made in United States
Troutdale, OR
03/04/2025